Steal Away

A FOLKTALE

by

Ramona K

SAMUEL FRENCH, INC.

25 WEST 45TH STREET   NEW YORK 10036
7623 SUNSET BOULEVARD HOLLYWOOD 90046
LONDON   *TORONTO*

CAST

(in order of appearance)

TRACYADA KYZER . . . . *Joyce Sylvester*
MRS. STELLA MARGARET KYZER . . . . . .* *Minnie Gentry*
MISS SUDY ATKINSON . . . . *Beatrice Winde*
MRS. RENITA (REDD) RUTH . . . . *Estelle Evans*
MRS. JADE LONG . . . .*Juanita Clark*
MRS. BLUIAH (BLU) DANIELS . . . . *Dorothi Fox*

*Appearing through the courtesy of Actor's Equity
  Association.

Time: Early 1930s

Place: Chicago

ACT ONE
    SCENE 1: Tracy's Homecoming Celebration
    SCENE 2: One Week Later
    SCENE 3: Two Weeks Later

There will be a ten minute intermission.

ACT TWO
    SCENE 1: Next Night, 10:00 P.M.
    SCENE 2: Later That Same Night

The action takes place in Stella Kyzer's home and The
Chicago Savings & Loan Bank.

5

STEAL AWAY

ACT ONE

SCENE 1

*For atmosphere, pre-show music should be gospel songs
of the period. They are also heard during blackouts
and scene changes.* TRACY *and* STELLA *are in* STELLA'S
bedroom dressing for the celebration. TRACYADA *is
staring idly out the window, thinking.* STELLA *enters
with snuff cup in her hand.*

STELLA. Tracy? Tracy? Good gracious! Is that as
far as you got? They'll be here any minute, you know
that. You best put some wings on them feet. I don't
want to have them waitin'.

TRACY. Grandmomma what I've got to say isn't
gonna take long. Let's just sit—

STELLA. —Now TracyAda I don't want no stuff out
you, specially today. Just finish dressing and close your
mouth. Don't tamper my heart.

TRACY. Grandmomma I know this may sound unus-
ual at first but . . . Momma you're not even listening to
me.

STELLA. You noticed. Now fool with me today hear?
I don't know what on earth you're plottin' this time and
I want to keep it just that way.

TRACY. But Momma these plans are all for the organization and everything you've fought and sacrificed
for.

STELLA. Hook this catch will you?

TRACY. The monies we get from my plan will all go
to support the organization

STELLA. Step out the way Tracy. And we don't need

7

no money. We got you through college didn't we? Didn't we?

TRACY. Yes but—

STELLA. —Pass me my handkerchief.

TRACY. Momma how long do you think all of you can continue that without all your funds drying up? Now I've been working on this for two years and—

STELLA. Tracy this is boring and besides you're gettin' on my nerves. Now I don't want you talkin' 'bout my organization anymore. When you get some sense maybe you can form your own, then you can do what you see fit. But right now take a comb to that head and get your cap and your gown. They'll be here any minute. Tracy I mean it, I don't want no stuff out you whatsoever and hand me my snuff cup.

(STELLA *EXITS to bathroom with the snuff cup. Upon hearing the bathroom door shut* TRACY *immediately goes into* HER *college chest and unravels a floor plan of the bank.* SHE *begins to study it.* SUDY *is entering the front door while knocking at the same time. The* WOMEN *carry paper bags and a gift wrapped book.*)

SUDY. (*Enters carrying a bag containing a "Welcome Home TracyAda" sign*) Stella? You whooo! We lettin' ourselves in.

STELLA. (*Sticks* HER *head out of bathroom door*) Make yourselves comfortable. I'll be there inside a minute.

BLU. Well the little rascal done graduated from college. A Amen and a Halloujah.

REDD. (*Enters carrying a cake*) You shouldn't talk 'bout Stella's grandchild like that.

SUDY. (SUDY *opens out a home-made "Welcome Home TracyAda" sign*) Now where'd we say this was going?

(The WOMEN are up decorating the front and dining room area. All except BLUIAH who sits down and blows balloons. The rest of the WOMEN are fussing about. This action continues until STELLA enters.)

BLU. *(Has found a chair and begins blowing balloons)* Shucks that's good news. If she can do it, nobody else should have trouble.

REDD. Let's hang it here.

SUDY. Rather proud of Tracy myself.

JADE. *(Sets out punch bowl)* We all are, considering her reports.

SUDY. Give me a hand Redd.

BLU. What reports?

JADE. Well, don't let this get no further, but I heard Tracy was handing out some papers.

BLU. Papers? What kind of papers?

SUDY. Right here is good.

JADE. Papers to rally up all the colored students. They were all supose to go and picket some ole store a colored women was turned 'way from.

BLU. See what I mean. Now don't that sound just like Miss TracyAda.

JADE. Tracy ought to know how dangerous that is.

SUDY. 'Specially in the South.

JADE. Why it wasn't but 2 weeks ago I heard of the Klu Klux Klan burning a cross at that family's home . . . the DeWitts for doing the self same thing.

REDD. Well, what we should be concerned about right now is the fact that she's graduated with a diploma and even some honors. And get your hands out my food. *(To BLU)*

JADE. Honors? Really?

REDD. That's right. Tracy got a high honor in science. The girl was way on up there at the top of her class. Even higher than the boys.

BLU. Science? We sending her to college to be a teacher.

SUDY. Well maybe she's gonna teach that science.

BLU. She better. I didn't save my hard earned cash for Tracy to be no doctor.

JADE. Just as long as she graduated. Now that's the important thing. I don't recall none of our other girls receivin' no honors. I sure hope my Charlotte can get an honor.

REDD. Speaking of the other girls. You know we're gonna have to start selling some more dinners at church. Our funds are swingin' mightie low.

BLU. I can't give no more money.

JADE. We all contributing what we can and I think we're gettin' by.

REDD. We're gettin', by strugglin'.

JADE. Well let's look forward to the celebration. I know a lot of church members didn't think we'd get thus far.

BLU. Sure didn't. But don't you know every other Sunday somebodies in my face talkin' 'bout their daughter being next. Talkin' mind you, with no money.

SUDY. Yes, but times is hard.

BLU. And harder on Colored folks.

REDD. That's why we should be thinkin' 'bout them dinners.

JADE. Well wonder what's keepin' the graduation queen?

(STELLA *ENTERS*)

STELLA. She's comin'.

JADE. Ohh don't we look nice!

STELLA. Thank you Sister Jade.

SUDY. Shinnin' today aren't you?

STELLA. Believe I have 'cause to.

SUDY. Shine on Sunbeam.

JADE. Did Miss Moses do your hair?

STELLA. No, I did it up myself. Was gonna let her touch it up 'cept I recalled the last time she yanked on it so, well you know she's going blind in one eye and can't half see out the other. And I just didn't feel like being yanked on today, so I fooled with it myself.

JADE. Well now, it come out lookin' real spiffy.

STELLA. I thank you again.

REDD. Stella, I think we all did a pretty good job decoratin' the joint. Don't you think?

BLU. Yeah we didn't do too bad.

SUDY. What you mean we?

STELLA. There's nothing like working and accomplishing together.

SUDY. That's right.

JADE. So where's the graduating queen?

STELLA. (*Raising her voice so* TRACY *can hear*) Tracy's coming. (TRACY *quickly rolls the map plan up and replaces it in the chest*) She's just primpin' up a bit.

SUDY. We only have an hour 'fore church reception.

JADE. Oh now Stella, don't let Tracy forget her cap and gown. Everybody wants to see her march down the aisle in her outfit.

BLU. Jade, Stella knows that.

JADE. Well Viola knew it too, but didn't she go on ahead and forget. And we had to hold up the ceremony for nearly 37 minutes while she ran home and got it. By time she finally got up to the platform she looked a nightmare. All her curls had done laid out and died and she was sweatin' like a rained on leaf. And who wants to listen to somebody talk about how educational they are looking like that. No, I don't think it hurts nothing to give a little gentle reminder.

STELLA. Thank you Jade.

JADE. See there.

REDD. Tracy! Is that you girl? Well looka here.

(TRACY *enters with* HER *cap and gown on her arm. The*

WOMEN *begin to fuss over* HER *as* SHE *goes about kissing each one.* STELLA *begins pouring punch from punch bowl, which has been brought in during the decorating.)*

JADE. Oh now don't we look sweet.

TRACY. Hello everyone.

(WOMEN *respond*)

BLU. Come here girl. Oh Stella she's fillin' out right nicely.

REDD. This just can't be the same little girl I used to sneak into movies.

STELLA. That's the one, always taggin' long after you.

(STELLA *begins to pass out glasses*)

REDD. Come here little Sister. I want me a big hug.

SUDY. Now let her come round here. Save me some sugar Tracy.

TRACY. It's so good to see y'all again.

BLU. You're home for keeps now. You'll be seeing us too much.

TRACY. I don't think that's possible.

REDD. Tracy we have something for you.

JADE. Yes Tracy, a gift.

TRACY. A gift? For me?

SUDY. It's just a little something, to show how much we appreciate you.

TRACY. Oh thank you.

JADE. Go on Tracy, open it.

TRACY. All right. Oh. Ah book. (*Reading*) A Guide To Elementary School Teaching. How nice.

BLU. See there. I told y'all Tracy didn't want no damn book.

SUDY. Well if it's agreeable let's get on with our ceremony. We don't have much time.

BLU. I second that.

REDD. Take center Sud.

SUDY. We the women of the Negro Women's Organization for Youth Education.

JADE. —in quicker terms known as the N.W.O.Y.E.

SUDY. Umm humm . . . division of the African Zionist Church—

JADE. —*independent* division of the African Zionist Church.

SUDY. would like to extend our deepest of congratulations to our third success, the now fully educated TracyAda. Raising Spirits and Heightening Pride. The Negro Women's Organization for Youth Ed—

JADE. —founded by our dear Stella Margaret Kyzer—

SUDY. Am I gonna do this or you?

JADE. Well it's important you get it right.

SUDY. Oh for Heaven sakes.

JADE. We don't ceremoney everyday.

REDD. Let her do it Jade.

JADE. Excuse me.

SUDY. Where was I?

JADE. —founded by Stella . . .

SUDY. who then chose special select members, which I'm very proud to be among. We're on our way to making this organization the success it is today. Why if it wasn't for Stell I don't know what would become of the educational future of our church youth. Now we—

BLU. You 'bout thru?

SUDY. I'm roundin' it up.

JADE. Patience is a virtue.

SUDY. So with the success that TracyAda has made for herself and the organization, we would like to welcome you as the newest member of the NWOYE and salute you, salute you, salute you.

BLU. Look out gut/hold on nose/open up mouth 'cause here she flows. (BLU *throws drink down* HER *throat*)

LADIES. (THEY *toast with a sip from their glasses*) Speech, Speech! Come on say something.

TRACYADA. Well I'm beyond grateful to you all, specially you Momma for supporting me. But also to all of you who have taken me into your hearts just like my Momma.

WOMEN. OHHHhhhh AHHHhhh.

TRACY. I really mean that. I have received my education but it is you have educated me. And knowing this has given me increased effort to achieve for you. I've been studying very hard over the past four years specially the last two. Thinking very seriously how Negro people must pull together. Not just a little, not just some of the time, but every waking hour we've got to be together in mind, body, spirit and soul.

REDD. That's right Tracy.

BLU. Go on girl.

TRACY. The NWOYE is accomplishing this. I'm honored to be surrounded by such loving women. You've given me so much. I salute you, as you salute me. Thank you Momma and to all my Mommas.

(*The* WOMEN *adlib their gratitude and hold their glasses up to toast once again.* THEY *then begin to move from their circle about the room.*)

JADE. Wasn't that just lovely.

REDD. Tracy you like to snatch a tear out my eye girl.

BLU. Cake! Cake! Ought to be a cake to slice after that.

STELLA. Hold your horses. It's comin' at you.

JADE. (*Is helping* STELLA *serve the cake. NOTE: Cake may be pre-cut*) Lord, Stell, you must be very proud.

STELLA. You know I am Jade. It's been a long time comin'. All my dreams and wishes blossoming in my child. Oh but pretty soon, you'll have your moment and Jade you'll know just what I'm feelin'. How old is Charlotte?

JADE. Two more years to go. Already counted.

STELLA. Shucks, that's no time. Look at Tracy, in one minute, out the next.

JADE. I 'magine you're right. I picture Charlotte graduating everytime one of our girls do. But with money being so tight, things just haven't got right yet since the depression.

STELLA. As long as we got the strength, we got the power. And when we get this bank loan next week, we'll have the money.

REDD. And the pies will be extra.

BLU. That's what the loan's for Redd. We trying to get away from them damn pies. Sweatin' my curls out . . .

SUDY. I don't mind tellin' y'all I'm a bit concerned 'bout this loan we askin' for, 'possin' we don't get it?

STELLA. Oh Ye of little faith.

JADE. Not to mention theses robberies occuring left and right. Stella you never know where these crookets gonna hit next.

REDD. That's why we should think about raising more funds with them pies. Since we're supposed to be so independent.

BLU. An opposin' view here. Besides the fact that I don't wish to sweat my curls out for those ungrateful so and sos. Dough and everything else is sky high. Folks are not going to pay the prices that we must charge in order to profit. That's in the first place. Now in the second place, if they don't buy, we're stuck with all them pies and no better ahead. We need something much surer than pies.

REDD. Such as?

BLU. I don't know yet.

REDD. We can't wait till you figure it out. Our funds are down. Something as to be done about it right now. Our goal in the beginning was to send at least one girl every year. We haven't been able to do that in the last two years, but with them pies—

BLU. Oh I don't want to hear nothin' else about pies.

JADE. You think all these bank robberies gonna affect the colleges?

REDD. Probably not.

JADE. Oh. Why not?

BLU. Ain't no banks at school.

JADE. That's a good reason, 'cept things have been gettin' so out of hand lately, I just don't know. Did you read where a copper got shot gettin' in the way of Dillenger, or was that the boy they call Baby Face Nelson?

TRACY. It was Dillenger.

JADE. All this shoot 'um up gives me the shakes—

BLU. —Well you brought it up.

SUDY. Then let's talk about somethin' pleasant, Jade!

STELLA. I got some news.

BLU. What's that?

STELLA. Odessa Johnsons' youngest got the calling.

SUDY. My stars.

BLU. You don't say.

REDD. Wasn't that the little rough girl used to pounce on Chester Jr.?

STELLA. That's her.

REDD. What ever congregation she preach for best not give her no lip.

BLU. Don't hear much about women preachers up-north. Let 'lone right here in Chicago.

SUDY. No, different cut of women.

JADE. That's nice. She got the future cut out for her already.

BLU. I suspect someone else got their future cut for

them too. Ain't that right Tracy?

TRACY. Excuse me?

REDD. You mightie quiet.

SUDY. But then they're runnin' their mouths like no tomorrow.

BLU. I said, what you gonna do now?

TRACY. Do?

SUDY. What school you plannin' to teach at?

TRACY. Teach? Oh. I haven't quite chosen it yet.

BLU. Well what you waitin' on Tracy?

JADE. I have an idea. Why don't you teach at your old grade school? They'd love to have you there. They only have two colored school teachers.

TRACY. Well I really hadn't thought about it.

BLU. Why not? You did go to school to be a teacher?

REDD. Well she don't have to teach at that school if she don't want to. Plenty other schools could use Negro teachers. Right Tracy?

TRACY. Yes, that's right.

JADE. Now I know you're going to have some kind of future to discuss at the reception.

STELLA. Who cares for more cake?

TRACY. Ahh, yes I will.

STELLA. (STELLA *snatches up* HER *plate and cuts more cake*) Redd?

JADE. Will what?

TRACY. Talk.

JADE. Well what is it that you're going to talk about Tracy? We'd all like to know what your plans are?

BLU. That's right, Tracy, money don't grow on trees and we'd like to know just what our monies going towards. So fess up.

STELLA. Ah, ah speaking of confessions. Doing my hair up like this reminds me of the days we used to shake a tail feather at the Sugar Shack.

SUDY. —with Jay McShann and how we use to get sharp as a tack. And the dances we used to do.

BLU. You dance?

STELLA. That's right smartie.

BLU. Can't imagine you dancin'.

SUDY. Is that so?

BLU. Yes that's so.

SUDY. Then do it Stell. Stella used to get on the floor and stop the show. Don't make me no fibber. Show 'em Stellie.

STELLA. Oh no I couldn't.

SUDY. Yes you can. Show her!

JADE. I want to see too. C'mon.

REDD. Yeah c'mon Stella, c'mon.

STELLA. Oh now we don't have time for that.

SUDY. Tap out a little somethin'. Show 'em you studied.

(SUDY *begins singing an old swing number. Perhaps "Sweet Georgia Brown."* THEY *all join in the singing urging* STELLA *on.*)

STELLA. Let me see now. (SHE *finds* HER *rhythm and begins tapping out a fluid old soft shoe. After a few bars and some fancy footwork,* STELLA *calls* BLU *to join* HER)

BLU. Oh yeah? Well look this over. (BLU *cuts a few steps of* HER *own. The* WOMEN *still sing. After a few dance steps* STELLA *and* BLU *end the dancing*) That's nice. And speaking of nice. It would be nice to know what you gonna do Tracy.

STELLA. Yes, we used to tap away just like this. (STELLA *goes at it again*)

SUDY. Sure did. (SUDY *begins singing again*)

BLU. Now listen y'all I want to know about this schoolin'. Tracy!

STELLA. (STELLA *snatches* BLU'S *plate*) May I help somebody to a second piece of chocolate cake?

JADE. —Oh yes that's right. What about it Tracy?

TRACY. I . . . I . . .

BLU. What's she mumblin' for?

REDD. I wish you'd leave her alone.

JADE. I should know what's going to be discussed at the ceremony. I want to know just how to introduce you.

TRACY. Well . . .

JADE. Go on.

REDD. Stop rushin' her.

TRACY. Well . . .

SUDY. Oh look at the time. I think—

BLU. —Hurry up Tracy.

TRACY. Well as I had ah previously mentioned . . . ah I ah while I was away at college many things came to light. I was thinking very hard about ah about ah the sit-situations of Negro people here in America and I thought that we as Negro women have been making miracles all our lives ah and the fact that all of the women present here are ah church women only serves to reenforce the beliefs we have in miracles ah because the Lord never tires of doing that job.

SUDY. Oh now she's gonna take us to church.

(SUDY *begins to hum "Leaning on the Ever Lasting Arms."* JADE *and* BLU *join in.*)

REDD. Hush! (THEY *don't*)

TRACY. And ah I was studying very hard and devised a plan so that we Negro women ah . . .

STELLA. TracyAda—

TRACY. —would be able to support our own ideas and ful-fil our goals even for the coming generations. Our sacrifices should not perish along with our lives.

REDD. Talk Tracy!

STELLA. TracyAda.

TRACY. So that's why the women under this roof would be the least suspects in recovering monies from the bank that is really ours to begin with.

(*The humming stops*)

BLU. Did anybody understand that?

STELLA. Well now, we should get going to the church—

JADE. —Tracy, I don't . . . I don't follow you.

REDD. Well ah wait a minute. Tracy walk with me. Now what you just said was that we should recover bank monies that's ours right? But no Tracy that can't be what you mean, 'cause that's be taking a bank. And that's not what you're saying?

BLU. Takin' a bank? Recoverin' money?

JADE. I didn't lose no money.

SUDY. And I keeps mines in the ice box.

BLU. Did I miss the punch line to this joke? Here we are toastin' this child out of college and she gon' to hell with herself.

STELLA. Watch out now Buelah Daniels—

SUDY. Tracy, I know you're not an average thinkin' child. Knew that first time I had you in church class. You even had ways of turnin' po' Jesus 'round, makin' him out to be a . . . What's that name you was forever calling him? A Revernedlutionist?

TRACY. A revolutionist. A soldier in the war on . . .

SUDY. How could I forget.

TRACY. He is a revolutionist if you really look at him. He made a complete change in the lives of people. He was nailed to the cross because of His beliefs—

BLU. And if you keep up this nonsensical talk somebodies gonna nail you to somethin'.

TRACY. Well at least I'll die for what I believe.

JADE. Oh now who said somethin' 'bout dying. If y'all talkin' 'bout that I better leave—

SUDY. And I don't hold no interest in being no criminal.

REDD. Oh Sudy!

SUDY. Well I don't!

REDD. All right now give the child a chance. Go 'head Tracy.

BLU. Give the child a who? That's what she got when she went to college. Ain't nobody standin' 'round here passing out chances.

STELLA. Blu Daniels watch yourself!

BLU. Sister Stella that's just what I'm plannin' on doing. I'm gonna watch myself walk out the door. Where's my piece of hat? Don't believe in disrespectin' nobodies roof.

SUDY. And I sure believed college would help that child. Looks like she's going off, just going deeper and deeper and . . .

TRACY. I supose within my excitement I didn't explain myself correctly. I'll start from the beginning.

BLU. No you won't. We late for reception as is—

JADE. (*Collects* HERSELF *to leave*—OTHERS *follow suit*)—Oh that's right, we still have to set up.

BLU. —and don't want to be later.

SUDY. Stella dear, rap a piece a cake for me, would you please?

BLU. Now Tracy, we holding this reception at church in your honor. Snap out it girl.

SUDY. Congratulations again Tracy. Let's see, that makes you the third student to graduate through our organization. Proud of you. Three Redd, three in my life time.

REDD. We're makin' history. And there'll be more and more.

SUDY. Thank you ma'm. (*Takes cake*) See you at church.

JADE. Very proud. Now Tracy you have 21 minutes left to make entrance. Don't forget anything.

BLU. (*Is at door*) Oh, by the way Mrs. Dillenger, meant to inquire. When we go sticking up these bank peoples, what should we use as weapons? Butterknives?

JADE. No, butterfingers.

(*The* WOMEN *EXIT in laughter*)

REDD. Tracy hold your point. (REDD *EXITS*)

(*The* WOMEN *have EXITED.* STELLA *is clearing away
some of the cake and rinsing or gathering the
glasses.*)

STELLA. Damnit to Hell TracyAda! Selfish. You
can't see nothin' least it's Tracy's plans, Tracy's ideas,
Tracy's concoctions. Everything has always been for
Tracy. One little piece of day, a torned off piece of
happiness that's all I ask and you can't let me have
that.

TRACY. I'm sorry, but what I've planned is vitally
important.

STELLA. When your foot drops the world don't tilt.
You pinchin' my last nerve girl.

TRACY. I know it came out wrong but—

STELLA. Now you listen. I only have one desire since
your graduation and that is for you to put all of this
nonsense aside. Don't you realize you can't survive on
this?

TRACY. After this I won't bring up another thing.

STELLA. I SAID NO! DAMNIT TRACY NO!

TRACY. Just once and it's over. Please Momma . . . ?

STELLA. You make me hate myself sometimes. Say
it damnit.

TRACY. Your organization isn't gonna last if we
don't do something to preserve its efforts.

STELLA. Just like your mother. Ada used to turn me
just like this.

TRACY. Momma . . .

STELLA. I know you don't remember Ada. But right
about your age she was becoming a little more sensi-
ble. You must be a late bloomer.

TRACY. Momma, if you really want to make an educational difference in the new generations then you,
we've got to send more than a handful of sisters to

college. But if its only 3 or 4 the way . . .

STELLA. If we can just send a handful we're doing something.

TRACY. Why send a handful when you can send more. Imagine, you started with 5 women growing into 500. It's very possible.

STELLA. Using me . . . You been using me Tracy. All them papers and articles you had me cutting up and mailing you. All them questions you had me asking. Two and two is just now making four. Every last one of them things you had me do had something to do with banks and timing and what have you. So this was the report you been studying on for two years. This was the report you needed so much help on. Not only did you use me but you lied to me as well. Who else been raising you Tracy? 'Cause all this ain't been instilled by me.

TRACY. I wanted to tell you. Momma I've come through this alone but only as far as I can. I can't do another thing without your help.

STELLA. No!

TRACY. I'll even find a husband, have babies, a blasted farm, but Momma right now I need you.

STELLA. So robbin' a bank is gonna do it? Come to earth Tracy. Ever hear of the FBI? Know what they do to Colored folks?

TRACY. Yes, but in order to protect ourselves, I planned that we'd take it off at night.

STELLA. Night? TracyAda!

TRACY. We got to. We have to use everything God gave us. We got color so we can mix with night. They won't even know we're out there. If we have something working in our favor we got to use it.

STELLA. Nobody rolls banks at night Tracy.

TRACY. Especially five Negro church women. Even the FBI would have a good laugh at the thought of five Negro church women robbin' a bank. Don't that sound peculiar? See how safe we are already. See

Momma we've got to plan for ourselves.

STELLA. But I wasn't plannin' on robbin' no bank. Do I have to remind you of the 8th commandment?

TRACY. It's not stealin' Momma. It's the same principle as the 40 acres and a mule. We were suposed to receive that to get started after reconstruction but never did. We were suposed to have the Bill of Rights protectin' us but they don't. The Proclamation of Emancipation don't stand for nothin' when we need it, so now we've come to collect.

STELLA. Lord deliver me. This is out and out craziness, so befittin' you Tracy. No!

TRACY. It's not crazy or impossible. What is impossible is that Negroes murder over arguing nickles. What is crazy is that we can work from can't see in the morning 'till can't see at night and won't have a thing to show for it 'cept another struggling generation. Momma try and see it with me. We can seize this bank and make it into a miracle for us. We can!

STELLA. Who you being now? Sojourner Truth or Robin Hood? No! I'm through speakin' up for you. Should have been through years ago. You want to take this up with the sisters, go right ahead. Miss Abolitionist. But don't expect me to say boo.

TRACY. You have to say something—

STELLA. No I don't! I've finally washed my hands. I'm tired Tracy. Now you get your cap and your gown, Stella wants to go. I know we have them waitin'.

(*As* TRACY *and* STELLA *collect* THEMSELVES *the* WOMEN *RE-ENTER.*)

JADE. See, I told you they'd be comin'. Now let's go.

REDD. Just wait we said we'd come back and at least listen.

SUDY. Well Tracy, we've all talked it over and decided that you oughta get another shot. Today's youth needs to be heard, even if what they got to say don't

make sense. We should least ways hear TracyAda out.
I 'magine you agreedin' too Stella.

BLU. I don't mind tellin' you I'm here against my
will . . .

JADE. Me too Tracy, 'cause this was gettin' me
pretty well nervous, talkin' 'bout dying and what not.
And once again I have to make an excuse . . .

REDD. All right Jade. We ready Tracy.

(STELLA *turns* HER *back*)

TRACY. Momma . . . ? I want to thank you all for
coming back and I wish to apologize for being selfish.
I know everyone worked so hard for this day—

REDD. —Including you.

SUDY. Stella, you feelin' all right?

BLU. We accept. Now what's the news?

TRACY. Well maybe I should tell you this some other
time and—

BLU. I'm not comin' back here for no more foolishness.

JADE. Yes Tracy, 'cause folks are gatherin' at church
so—

BLU. Say it and let's get a move on 'cause I'm not
comin' back.

SUDY. Take your time child.

TRACY. I . . . I was gonna tell this some other way.
I got too excited before and when I get excited I mess
up. In my second year of college I took up psychology.
Which I had a report to do on. The professor handed
out a list of townspeople who volunteered every year.
My finger landed on a man named Pine. I introduced
myself to a down home colored gentleman. He rattled
on 'bout hisself without me even asking one question.
When he got through, I told him he didn't tell me
nothing that I didn't already know about Colored folks.
Pine said all right Miss College, some folks might take
me for a 93-year-old criminal. Pine told me when he

was a youngin' his folks owned this land. Almost just
the way I saw it then. It took 3 to 4 hours to see it
all by horse. Pine said times were different when he
was coming up. Colored folks had them some land. Not
no little bitty somethin' but he meant land. But wasn't
for long white folks began building and movin' closer
towards the colored settlement. They wanted to run a
railroad train right on through the colored parts.
They were going to bunch 'em up into one little spot.
All the Negro folks got together to talk to the mayor.
They talked and talked till it was evident that this
train was to run straight through 52 colored front
rooms regardless. His folks and a handful of families
felt no matter what this just wasn't worth giving up
their farming and homes. 'Bout seven whites came
after his Pa. He sat right on the front porch, rifle
restin' in his lap and said, if you take my home you're
gonna have to take me first. There were words and
before his Pa died he took care of four and his wife
shot one. All Pine had was 10 years of life, a gun, and
both folks dead. It was then that he promised may God
thrash him to Hell if he didn't come back and get his
folks land. When I met him he was sittin' on it. Every
tree he placed just the way he remembered it some 80
years back. Trains didn't last. They kept messing up
when coming through them 52 front rooms. Word car-
ried it was jinxed. Got so people didn't want to ride
no further than the stop before the colored section. So
that land was to be sold for what the railroad termed
a "steal." But when they saw Pine they doubled the
price. So Pine worked on a plan to get money out the
bank round the same time as the Jessie James and
Cole Younger bands were robbing. He pulled it off at
night so he wouldn't be recognized. They never found
out. When he goes he's giving his land to the school.
He said we got to provide for each other. Or else every
generation has to start from scratch. Then Pine asked
me what was I gonna do? I couldn't bring myself to

say a word, 'cause I didn't know. But from that moment I knew I had to organize this mission. Something that would do for us what Pine's had done for him. That's when I changed my studies and took up science and mathematics. This would aid me in constructing the floor plans of the bank along with its timing and alarm system. I could through research teach myself the technical operation of vaults. It was very difficult. But I learned. I thought about Pine and I learned. Now, if one man can carry a burden for 50 years and make a miracle out of it, what you think 5 women can do? Pine said God would be with you as long as your heart is in the right place. We can do it. But it's now up to y'all, 'cause I'm ready.

JADE. Did Pine say he had help when he robbed that bank?

TRACY. No.

JADE. Maybe you won't need none neither.

BLU. You mean to tell me we came back here for this?

TRACY. I wish you'd think about what I've got planned.

JADE. I wish you'd think about what I've got planned. I refuse to make another speech like the Viola one. So just come on young Miss.

SUDY. Well we did come back.

TRACY. Wait a minute—

JADE. I can just picture everybody seated and sweatin'. Next thing they'll do is drink up the refreshments. And now that Bluiah went and told her bar friends we were serving food, we'll have more folks than we can handle.

BLU. I didnt' tell nobody we were serving food.

JADE. Maybe you didn't. Much as you like to eat, you probably want it all for yourself. (SHE *EXITS*)

BLU. Say what? (BLU *EXITS following* JADE)

REDD. It's not a bad plan Tracy, it just ain't for us. (SHE *EXITS*)

SUDY. It's gettin' late Stella.
STELLA. And she still ain't come 'round.

(THEY *EXIT leaving* TRACY *center stage*)

—*BLACK OUT*—

ACT ONE

SCENE 2

One week later.

BLU *is dancing around with herself.* SUDY *and* JADE *are bustling back and forth from the kitchen wrapping up pies and rolls to be delivered.* TRACY *is in her bedroom reviewing her papers from her chest. The song on radio is a Louis Armstrong piece.* BLU *takes a flask from her purse, pours herself "a shot" in the flask cup, puts in away and continues dancing.*

SUDY. Bluiah why don't you turn that down and help?
JADE. Ain't it the truth. I can't hear myself think.
BLU. That's 'cause you ain't thinkin' 'bout nothin'.
BLU. Listen to that Louis Armstrong. He sure can play with his colored self. Wonder if that son of a gun is married?
JADE. I think so.
BLU. Wonder if he's gettin' divorced?
JADE. I think not.
BLU. I remember when I saw him in New Orleans, during my travelin' days. Talk 'bout charming. Why if

I wasn't a lady, I'd a done like the rest of 'em.

SUDY. What's that?

BLU. I'd a numbered my draws and pitched 'em at him.

JADE. Good thing you didn't.

BLU. Why?

JADE. Yours might have landed and killed him.

BLU. All right Jade.

JADE. When's Stella gettin' in?

SUDY. She oughta be breezin' in soon. Tracy! Tracy!

TRACY. Yes Ant Sudy. (TRACY *quickly puts* HER *papers in chest*)

SUDY. Give us a hand sugar. Since Miss Bluiah is intent on dancin' herself dizzy.

TRACY. Coming!

BLU. Me and these pies ain't gon' make it.

JADE. Bluiah c'mon.

BLU. I sincerely hope Stella gets a great big loan.

JADE. Redd oughta be comin' with them orders soon. Then you can get on outta here and deliver them.

BLU. I'm not burning up anymore of my gas delivering them pies. Gas went up to 15 cents last week.

SUDY. Oh you'll deliver them all right.

TRACY. Here I am.

SUDY. Help Jade. (*To* TRACY)

JADE. (*Hands* HER *a pan of rolls from kitchen*) Don't drop my rolls.

SUDY. I suggest we start deciding who we're going to send to college this year.

BLU. Second the motion.

JADE. There were five, but Bessy swallowed the watermelon seed and you know Simara's mother passed and she has to be mother to them boys. So that makes do with Marie Turner's girl Elzatie, Mrs. Flowers' child Annie, and that little wild puss they call "Puff."

SUDY. Puff?

BLU. You know Eugene's daughter, Pen-a-lope.

JADE. No Penelope.

SUDY. That clears up why they call her Puff.

JADE. We could nominate Annie.

BLU. Why?

JADE. Do I have to have a reason?

SUDY. It would help Jade.

JADE. She's a good girl. 'Tends church regularly.
Don't hear no fresh talk out her mouth and she's gonna
make somethin' out herself mark my word. Do us real
proud we chose her.

BLU. We could nominate Puff.

JADE. Why?

BLU. 'Cause she's a bad girl. 'Tends church on
Easter only, got a fresh mouth, shows her panties to
the boys and if we don't make something out her she
might not think to do it herself. And that would be a
shame too, 'cause everybody knows she's a wizard, but
don't nobody ever give her the chance.

JADE. That's 'cause she's too busy showin' off her
panties. We all work too hard to be throwin' our
money away on someone like her. 'Sides I don't think
the organization needs to send nobody like that to
college.

BLU. Let's face it Jade, sometimes you don't think
period. Now we done sent some sweetie pies already.
It's time to mix it up a bit. 'Course we ain't countin'
Tracy she's mixed up as it is.

SUDY. All right Blu.

TRACY. What about Elzatie?

BLU. Elzatie don't want to go to college. Her
mother's shovin' that on her.

SUDY. May I throw my 2 cents in the kitty?

BLU. Take center.

SUDY. Granted, the point of our organization is to
send sisters to school, but let's think of catchin' two
feathers with one swipe by including girls that haven't
had the support that others have had. Perhaps with a
gesture like this we could get them pokin' in another
direction.

TRACY. That's true. Remember when you told me, when Jesus chose his 12 none of those men were saints. They all had some kind of record of weakness.

SUDY. That's right daughter. If we could use the insight the Lord bestowed us with maybe we can find treasures gone inside a person. Goodness should not pass unrewarded, but it's where there's no one at all that the heart should extend itself that would be saying something for the organization. What do you think? Let's not waste time. If Stella and Redd agrees it'll be Puff. Then whose gonna ask her?

TRACY. Why don't you do it Miss Jade?

BLU. Second that motion.

JADE. Now you're twistin' my arm.

BLU. Ahh go on Jade you heard fresh talk before.

JADE. If that child gives me any back sass, I'll belt her one.

BLU. That's the right spirit for our future generation.

SUDY. I propose next week each of us will have slept on the idea of raising funds. I know 'bout this thing called depression, it's just another of them obstacles we gon' have to punch out. "Progress" is what we're after. So let's come back with some usable suggestion. And that includes you now Tracy.

TRACY. Yes ma'm.

BLU. I second, but no pies.

JADE. I just thought of something.

SUDY. What's that?

JADE. How 'bout us having a baby contest?

BLU. Oh who wants to be foolin' with a bunch of brats?

SUDY. Folks do love the little ones. Draw it up and bring it next week.

JADE. Oh goodie.

BLU. For Heavens sakes.

(REDD *ENTERS*)

JADE. I thought you got lost.
SUDY. Well who wants what?
BLU. What's wrong with your face?
REDD. We got a lot of cancellations.

(WOMEN *respond*)

BLU. Who? (REDD *hands her the list*)
REDD. Too many to say.
SUDY. Well what happened?
BLU. All of these cancelled?
REDD. In a nut shell, folks can't afford them any-more.
JADE. But I thought—
REDD. We were all thinkin' wrong. Maybe if we sold them cheaper.
BLU. Can't get no cheaper than what we're asking. We giving 'em away as is. Didn't I tell you we can't profit off no pies.
TRACY. What are we going to do with all this food?
SUDY. Oh Lord.

(THEY *pause and ponder* THEIR *situation.* STELLA *ENTERS and marches towards her bedroom visibly shaken*)

SUDY. Hey Buddy.
JADE. Stella I'm so glad you got here we—
BLU. What's wrong with Stella?
REDD. ... something.
SUDY. (SUDY *intercepts* STELLA) Stella ... Stella ... ?
TRACY. Momma? What's wrong Momma?
SUDY. Somebody get her a glass of water.
STELLA. Get me some spirits.
SUDY. Come sit honey.
REDD. What happened?
STELLA. They turned us down. They thought it was

a joke that we put in for a loan. Mr. Greyson told me
we couldn't be serious. He laughed at me. I asked him
for the loan again and he laughed at me. I even told
him I'd put my home up for calateral. Not only did he
tell me it wasn't good enough, but he laughed in my
face. Told me colored children didn't need no education. That he didn't have any money to be giving away
on colored education. He said famers needed money to
buy pigs. He laughed. Then he got up from his desk
and one by one every worker in that bank shot their
eyes at me, snickering. He said, why don't you go on
home Auntie and let us decide whose to be educated.
It was all I could do to restrain myself. Short ones, tall
ones, thin ones, even had their children red faced and
laughing at me. I thought I knew what Jesus felt,
carrying his cross to the mountain. I didn't know
nothin' till I felt that laughter on my back. On my
back out the door, on my back in the streets. People
laughing. Making fun of this po' Auntie Stella. Now
I know, I know what Jesus felt. They got a lotta ways
of spittin' on ya.

(*The* WOMEN *are stunned to silence by* STELLA'S *words.*
    Absently THEY *reflect*)

REDD. Colored folks don't need education—
JADE. Farmers need pigs and we don't need . . .
BLU. I'll just be damn. So educating our girls don't
mean nothin' to him. Never mind that we provided
for the education of Viola and Tracy, that don't mean
a thing to him. We're a joke.
REDD. We need that money.
SUDY. I tell you, I feel like going back to that
bank—
STELLA. —and taking that money.
SUDY. Will we always be ignorant colored folks to
them?

TRACY. Until we prove we're not—yes.

(*Pause*)

REDD. The N.W.O.Y.E. needs that money y'all. We need it . . .

(*The pause again this time with the realization of what* TRACY *has said*)

SUDY. Well then . . . Tracy . . . what about them plans you been working on?

TRACY. I've compiled everything we have to know.

REDD. Well then Tracy you have to teach us 'bout this bank stuff 'cause we don't know much on it.

SUDY. If God protected a crazy like Mister Pine, maybe he'll protect a baby like you and fools like us.

TRACY. I intend for us to take what we came for as quickly as possible and leave, unnoticed. That's why we're going to take it off at night.

BLU. Night?

JADE. You can't see nothin' at night.

TRACY. I know.

STELLA. She means there's less of a danger at night. Less of being seen, less of being caught—

BLU. And less of not knowing what the hell I'm doing.

JADE. How we gonna know what we're doing in the dark.

REDD. Well now I can think of lots of things we do in the dark and we know exactly what we're doing.

BLU. Case closed.

TRACY. Our advantage to this entire mission is that bank robberies are happening right now in this area. When we hit and we've got to do it now, our mission will be swept right in with the other bank robberies. No one will suspect us. They'll finger Dillinger, Floyd even Baby Face Nelson, but never us.

REDD. Listen to that girl.

TRACY. There's only one thing that I must have and that is that you trust me and each other completely. If we have that we can accomplish.

SUDY. Amen.

REDD. Yes.

BLU. Fine.

TRACY. I'll get the plans. (SHE *EXITS to bedroom*)

SUDY. (*The* WOMEN *gather around* STELLA) Stella, you heard your child as well as we did. What do you say?

STELLA. We have always honored majority rule.

REDD. We know that Stella, but we want to know what you think?

BLU. You're stalling Stell. What is it?

TRACY. (*RE-ENTERS*) We're ready. Is there a problem? (*No answer*) Then let's gather around the table. (*The* WOMEN *hesitatingly begin gathering around the table.* ALL *except* STELLA) You are coming Momma? (SHE *does not move*)

BLACKOUT

ACT TWO

SCENE 1

Three weeks later.

Scene opens with the WOMEN *seated and standing about the dining and front rooms.* STELLA, SUDY *and* BLUIAH *are cleaning their guns.* JADE *is sewing on a pair of men's suit pants.* REDD *is studying the bank plans on the table.* TRACY *is pacing the room nervously.*

TRACY. Time?

REDD. 7:58.

TRACY. We can begin. What do we have Redd?

REDD. (*Reading from ledger*) The schedule reads as follows: A—Tonight we'll clean weapons, B—Organize our equipment, C—Practice drills, and D—Run down the take.

TRACY. We may commence with the evening. Issue procedures.

REDD. All right women, we shall start the night by loading our weapons, then by cleaning and checking.

(JADE *quietly sneaks off to the bathroom*)

TRACY. Thank you Redd. Momma is everything packed?

STELLA. Solid as a rock.

TRACY. And you're positive of where everything is located.

STELLA. (*Without looking* SHE *feels inside the bag*

for instruments) Without looking for it either. Here
are the snippers, flashlight, money bags and the stethoscope.

TRACY. Good. Where's Jade?

SUDY. In the toilet.

REDD. She's developed this peeing condition since we
got deep into the plans.

BLU. That's all we need.

SUDY. Maybe she'll pull out of it.

BLU. She just better. We only got 'till tomorrow
night and she sure as hell can't use the bank's toilet.
Wouldn't that be nothin'. Here we all got the loot doing a soft shoe out the bank and somethings missing
—Jade. We about face to find, not her, but that ole
distance sound of the toilet flushin'. Now that's all the
cops would have to do is hear her flushin' the toilet
and come cuff us up. It's make headline news. "THE
TOILET WAS KEY LEAD IN ARRESTIN' COL-
ORED GROUP" or better still "COLORED WOMEN
GETS CAUGHT FLUSHIN' TOILET." Now I ask you
wouldn't that be a blip? I'm gonna put a suggestion in
right now. As protection measure, we best hook up
something for Miss Jade. Bring a potty or put our
hands together and cup, somethin'. But don't I repeat
don't let her flush no toilets. Or we'll be poppin' them
rocks with the chain gang. I have an idea there's more
to her condition anyway.

TRACY. How you makin' out Ant Sudy?

SUDY. Pretty well I thank you. Matter fact, sneaks
back old memories.

STELLA. Don't it though? Don't believe I've cleaned
a gun since Mister Kyzer passed.

SUDY. Tracy you wasn't round yet, but your grandpaps used to bring home possum every year on Stella's
birthday. Didn't miss a one did he Stella?

STELLA. 'Till the morning he passed?

SUDY. You ain't never had possum way Mister Kyzer
fixed it up. Girl, it make you want to sing. Jade could

tell you, so could Blu if she wanted to.

BLU. Never mind Miss Sudy.

SUDY. Blu used to have eyes for your grandpaps.

TRACY. You did?

STELLA. Sudy!

SUDY. Oh Stella it don't make no never mind now.

SUDY. But your grandpaps was pure gentlemen. Blu was too wild. He ain't take to them wild women. 'Sides Stellie here would have skinned his behind along with Miss Blu here if something were to make of it.

BLU. Ain't worth it.

SUDY. See there. But Stellie kept her sleeves rolled up.

STELLA. But that 'possum sure was nice.

SUDY. Surely was. I used to go 'coon huntin' myself Tracy.

TRACY. 'Coon huh?

SUDY. Future Negro women don't know much on that.

BLU. Them some garbage pickers. If you ever hear something like fighting cats, that's coons talkin' in the night.

SUDY. See I was the oldest child, being there were no boys, I had to do what a son might do and that's go huntin' with my Pa. And child it can't get near as dark here like the nights in Beauford. Woo! Gets so dark colored peoples just smooth right on in with night.

REDD. Sounds like West Viriginia.

TRACY. Weren't you scared?

SUDY. First three times I wet myself.

STELLA. No you didn't Sudy.

SUDY. But I wouldn't tell Pa. I'd go whistin' right on along like everything's peaches. But real short after that I decided not to get scared no mo'. 'Cause travelin' round in damp drawers, in that night air with the wind singing all up your legs, ain't a bit of fun. I got over my fright, fast. Coon meant crops, seed, food. Meant nobody was forced to skip meal. I know one thing, I can still do it if I had to.

REDD. Well now, that's the only way to be. Y'all oughta be glad I'm sure too.

SUDY. Why's that?

REDD. Due to my ric-a-che talent you can feel extra safe in my company.

SUDY. Ric-a-che talent, is that a fact?

REDD. In the old West I had me a reputation for knockin' down two bandits with one bullet.

SUDY. No foolin'?

REDD. For sure honey. (REDD *does whirling number with* HER *gun*) Now sit on that.

STELLA. Didn't know you were fancy Miss Redd.

REDD. Fancy? Shucks, that's my middle name. Oh that's right y'all didn't know me when I was Queen of the West.

SUDY. Reckon we didn't Miss Redd.

STELLA. Did we miss something?

REDD. 'Course you did. For instance, if word got out that I was comin' through, townsfolks would vacate rather than tangle with Miss Redd.

SUDY. Oh go on.

STELLA. You don't say.

REDD. I do. There I'd be struttin' in town with that look in my eye. I'd spot me the wrong doer, and I'd say DRAW, 'cause your life depends on it—Buster.

(TRACY *EXITS looking for* JADE)

STELLA. Women too?

REDD. Miss Redd ain't had no sympathy.

STELLA. And all this by your lonesome?

REDD. It was a lonely life, but my only life.

STELLA AND SUDY. Ummmmmmmmmmmmmmmm.

BLU. Now all this might have been dependin' if Daniels wasn't available. You all weren't famaliar with me when I was known as DANIELS OF DIRTMOUTH MISSISSIPPI and wasn't to be fooled with.

(*The* WOMEN *quickly put their guns down and face off. They use their hands and fingers as guns.*)

SUDY. Da da da da. So it 'twas womens and gentle-
mens, Daniles from Dirtmouth and Redd from Fire-
butt Tenessee, met up one cold and windy evenin' in
Hopeing to Live Lousianna. Theys come to battle it
out for the honor to be, Queen of the South. And this
is just 'bout how it happened way back when. Da da
da daaaa.

BLU. (*Has ran behind a chair*) All right Miss Redd,
I'm being polite, give yourself up or say your prays.

REDD. Yous the one better fall on them knees. I got
me a bullet here with your name on it, BUELAH
DANIELS!!

BLU. Ha! That and a horse'll get you to the next
town. Now don't force me to come after you girl. Just
come on out with them hands high. Save your Momma
some sorrow.

REDD. Momma...? My Momma? She did say my
Momma?

STELLA/SUDY. Yep! Girl you in a heap of trouble
now. That done did it.

BLU AND REDD. BOOM BOOM BANG BOOM. (*The
guns sounds continue half-way through* SUDY'S *lines*)

STELLA. SOS they fought it out just like I said.
Well the townsfolks was shiverin' 'hind drawn shades.
Cussin' themselves for not catchin' the first thing
smokin'. Night was comin' round the bend. Sky was
turnin' Negro Black with stars sinkin' in fast. Then,
the boom booming ceased. Got quiet like for a spell.
All of a big sudden this voice, this tired worn out
voice a puffin'—

BLU. I—I ain't got no more bullets.

SUDY/STELLA. Poor child.

REDD. Well I do and it's the one that got your name
on it.

SUDY/STELLA. Da da da daaaaa.

REDD. Let it be known I gave you opportunity to
save yourself. Now it's too late. Bye. (REDD *"shoots"*
BLUIAH *and* SHE *falls out*)

BLU. (*Pops back up*) Let it be also known I fought the good fight. Y'all just remember my name—Blu Daniels from Dir—Dirtmouth Mis—(REDD *shoots* HER *again*)

REDD. BoOM! I said bye. Now you're dead, you understand Dead.

BLU. Yous right I'm dead but first—

REDD. Will you die already—

BLU. Just a second I got to get this right.

REDD. When's she gonna die? (*Turning to* STELLA *and* SUDY) That's just why I don't like to fool with colored folks. They don't know when to give up.

BLU. You just can't 'ppreicate some down home actin'.

REDD. Actin' the fool you mean.

BLU. I'll have you know I starred in a church play when I— (*There is noise at the bathroom door and* JADE *fumbles to get out.* BLU *goes for a stick.* BLU *stands to side of bathroom door*) —was a little girl and I sang too. Used to bring rivers to the old folks eyes I— (JADE *and* TRACY *RE-ENTER,* TRACY *first.* JADE *comes out and* BLU *sticks* HER *in the back pretending to have a gun*) —All right Miss Jade, we takin' you in for sewing up gangster outfits! Get them hands up, higher, higher!! (BLU *tickles* HER)

JADE. Buelah stop it, now just stop it! My nerves are weak as it is.

BLU. Sos your bladder.

JADE. Don't fool with me Buelah Daniels. I'm in no kind of mood to be tampered with. Just keep off my nerves.

BLU. Ah now just calm down Sister. We all got the shakes. And that don't give you no reason to be any more cranky than the rest of us. You better pull yourself together. 'Course, now if the real problem is Zeke, you'll just have to tell him to leave you alone.

STELLA. Blu!

JADE. Who said anything 'bout my husband? I didn't say a word 'bout him being no problem, that's you puttin' words in my mouth.

BLU. Oh now just calm down Sister. Ain't never been no secret 'bout you and your husband.

SUDY. My Stars!

JADE. And it ain't never been no secret 'bout you and Mamie's husband, but I don't go round publicizing it. Do I?

BLU. That's 'cause Mamie's husband don't bounce me round like your husband do. Now if it 'twere me, I'd take a brick and settle Zeke's nerves.

JADE. That's it! You done tore your drawers now. Who you think you're talkin' to? Stand up Blu sos I can knock you down. Had 'nuff of your foolishness. Come on get up! (JADE *is bouncing around* BLU *with both fists up*) Get up yellow belly, get up!

BLU. Now what she look like?

TRACY. Jade, Blu that's enough.

JADE. It's gonna be what you look like when I land on you.

STELLA. Jade now come on—

JADE. No no Stella. I'm gonna fix her mouth so she can learn to talk right in it.

REDD. Blu why don't you apologize?

BLU. For tellin' the truth?

JADE. I'm doing the count down when I hit on zero you gonna see stars.

REDD. Go head!

SUDY. Stubborn as a jackass.

JADE. 3.

BLU. All right Jade.

JADE. 2!

REDD. Hope you do see stars!

JADE. Windin' up!

TRACY. Blu!

JADE. And—

BLU. I'm sorry. Now what?

JADE. Don't favor how you said that, plus one-half and—

BLU. I'm sorry Jade, please forbid me.

JADE. Just as smart as 2 dumb rabbits.

STELLA. All right now y'all.

TRACY. Can we get settled? This has taken a lot of work and commitment on your part. Maybe we needed what happened. But understand we don't need any of that from now until tomorrow night. Now let's move on. Redd shall we go through the drill?

REDD. Women put it together now.

SUDY. Never had it apart.

REDD. ATTENTION! HUP HUP HUP / HUP / HUP / HUP AND RIGHT FLANK MARCH! TO THE REAR MARCH! TO THE REAR MARCH! DOUBLE TO THE REAR TO THE RIGHT FLANK MARCH HALT! (JADE *fumbles each command*) Well we didn't do too bad considerin' (*Looks at* JADE) Well done women.

JADE. I don't know why we have to go through this all the time. I never get it right.

TRACY. So you can get your blood circulating and your thoughts moving. Discipline. Now if we will gather round, we'll go through these plans for the last time. (*The* WOMEN *gather around the table*)

JADE. This is it huh?

TRACY. There's nothin' to fret over. We've all gone over your part a thousand times.

JADE. How 'bout one mo'?

TRACY. No. We've got to stay on schedule. Before we run the take, you should know the mission has been running smoothly. We're on schedule and in excellent shape for tomorrow night.

BLU. We're going through with it aren't we?

TRACY. Let's run down the take.

BLU. Aren't we?

TRACY. I said, let's run the take.

REDD. I'm not doubting Thomas, but Jade are you

positive you know just how to do with them wires?

JADE. If I told you once I told you half dozen times.

TRACY. We've been through this.

REDD. Well let's be through it again. I need to know.

TRACY. For what? We've all seen Jade work. For that matter we've all watched each other work. And Redd you of all have seen her. Why the questions now?

REDD. I saw her work before her peeing condition, this throws a new light on the subject. What Blu said ain't all that off. Supposin' she does get so nervous she has to use the toilet. We can't offer to pack another thing to wipe up any traces. Now this is serious.

JADE. What traces? What'd y'all say when I wasn't here?

BLU. Well maybe we'll diaper her.

JADE. You don't value your life, do you?

TRACY. Now wait a minute. We know what we have to do there's no reason to panic. We can't afford to do that.

REDD. I can. It may be my last time in life to panic. Just bear in mind who you planned to come out last that's all.

TRACY. You're not the last one out, I'm with you.

REDD. What's that mean?

TRACY. It means I'll be with you. Whatever happens to you happens to me too.

REDD. And that's just what I'm afraid of. You're ready right now to give up your right arm for this mission. I'm just realizin' you've decided all along if something should happen to you it's all right. Tracy-Ada it ain't by no means all right if something happens to me. Being that the case, what you think a person like you and I got in common if and when the going gets tough?

TRACY. If we don't panic the going will not get tough. This will work. What's wrong with you Redd? You didn't feel like this before?

REDD. Before is before, I'm talking now. Right this minute.

JADE. Well now all y'all can snicker 'bout me but you're not two blinks from wettin' your own pants.

REDD. I don't need that.

JADE. And I did?

BLU. Yes you did.

JADE. Shut up Buelah.

REDD. It's because of you I'm worried now.

JADE. Because of yourself you mean. Put it where it belongs.

REDD. I can take care of myself, thank you.

JADE. And I told you I know what to do, thank you. Now whose peeing?

SUDY. Alla y'all.

BLU. Redd, you're not the only one alone. 'Least Tracy's with you, whatever that means, I'm in the car all by my lonesome.

SUDY. You ain't half as alone as I am, but I'm not complainin'.

BLU. Maybe you don't have sense enough to know you could possibly die.

JADE. Now I got to go to the bathroom. (*Starts to EXIT is stopped by* SUDY)

SUDY. I said before if I had to stay alive I could. Seems like you the one done forgot.

BLU. I ain't even forgot.

SUDY. Must have if you using that tone on me.

BLU. Oh now we gonna talk 'bout speech patterns.

REDD. I'm not through Tracy.

JADE. You oughta be.

REDD. This is all your fault, you know that don't you? Got us workin' like dominos. If we do right we're on. If one person messes up we're all off.

JADE. Well y'all never heard me say this was a good idea.

BLU. Always stirrin' in the devil with your plans.

STELLA. Hush now.

JADE. I always felt this was up to no good.

STELLA. Stop it.

BLU. You know I did, but I was just going along with the rest—

REDD. I never thought we'd have to use guns—

JADE. But I figured for my Charlotte I'd go—

STELLA. Shut up damnit! Shut up! I won't have you attacking her like dogs. I won't have it. So your back-bones done slipped. Well it ain't nobodies fault but your own. We got a commitment, a deadline and work to do. But if we no longer hold to that, then let's decide it right this minute. Are we going through with this or not?

JADE. Stella I was just—

STELLA. We doing it or not? If we're not, leave. If we are, say it for once and for all. Well? Talk?

BLU. I want out. I didn't think we'd get this far. I feel like something's gonna go wrong. It's better to be free and strugglin' than in prison unable to do any-thing.

REDD. Maybe she's right.

JADE. I'm not used to any of this. But I'll do any-thing for my Charlotte, anything. She's the only baby I had that lived, and I want to see her graduate. But I don't want to back out, 'less others do.

BLU. I want out. (BLUIAH *moves to leave*)

SUDY. Buelah sit.

BLU. You don't rule me.

SUDY. Ain't nobody in this room turnin' back. Give yourself a minute to understand what I'm saying. Now sit.

(BLUIAH *returns to table and sits*)

STELLA. Say what we gotta do Tracy.

TRACY. I'm sorry that—

STELLA. —that ain't it.

TRACY. Back to the ledger. Renita.

REDD. Third and last on agenda: Run down the take.

TRACY. For the last time, we'll do it by map. I want to emphasize the importance of fixin' a picture in your mind of the bank. Even though the vault is in the open, it's all going to be different in the dark. It's our memory that's gonna keep us on schedule. And the schedule will make us or break us. All right the clock's tickin'—Blu!

(*The* WOMEN *lean over map.* EACH *pointing* HER *individual task*)

BLU. I've driven us to bank, cars parked in front of Tom's Pharmacy at the corner. I wait.

SUDY. I cover the alley way while y'all enter back of the bank. Then I stand guard.

JADE. I cut alarm wires. Deaden system. We're in.

REDD. I lead the way, flashlight in hand. Take up look out post in front window.

STELLA. We're at the vault, I hand Tracy the stethoscope.

TRACY. Stethoscope on, I crack the safe.

STELLA. Money bags out, we're loading.

JADE. Passing down to Redd.

TRACY. I clean up.

REDD. I lead way out.

SUDY. I signal to Blu.

BLU. I roll to alley.

SUDY. Cover for them to car.

BLU. Drive back to Stellas.

TRACY. Keep going.

REDD. Once in house all suits removed.

STELLA. I collect the money bags.

TRACY. I collect suits for burning.

REDD. When we're all clothed the mission is accomplished.

TRACY. It's as cut and dry as that. If we panic,

we'll kill each other. Recover your confidence and we will be fine. We will. Questions? No eating or drinking after 7 p.m. Get only the rest you need. Report here as you would for the NWOYE. Don't be late. Nervous is one thing, panic will kill us. *Questions?*

REDD. You think we could spill some together Stella?

(STELLA *gets out* HER *bootleg and glasses. As* SHE *pours* SUDY *talks.*)

SUDY. Comfort. That's all we need. Just a bit of comfort. Don't know where that might be for y'all, but since my huntin' days, comfort been just one special star. Pappy used to say, Sudy find yourself a star and it will never leave you. Even if you get lost, just member that star and go on back to where you started out. That's what Jesus put stars in the sky for. Light the way, find the way back to ourselves.

(*The* WOMEN *embrace one another and EXIT.*)

SUDY. It's gonna be all right.
STELLA. It will have to be won't it?
STELLA. Night ole buddy.
SUDY. Good night darlin'.

(SUDY *EXITS*)

TRACY. Need some help Momma?
STELLA. (*Begins gathering her glasses and replaces bootleg*) Don't you think tonight you should hit the bed early yourself?
TRACY. I plan to. Just have to go over this one more time.
STELLA. That's what you said last night and night 'fore that one.
TRACY. After this I'm comin'.
STELLA. You're not short on faith are you?

TRACY. What do you mean?

STELLA. You were having a bad dream again last night. I figured you didn't know about them.

TRACY. No. And it doesn't matter.

STELLA. It's the bigger person that can admit when he's wrong.

TRACY. Now whose short on faith?

STELLA. Who you sassin'?

TRACY. I been looking at you too Momma. You haven't gotten in my way, but you sure don't help me like you used to.

STELLA. Best get accustom.

TRACY. I wish you'd understand that this mission is bigger than the differences we have. It's just more vitally important.

STELLA. You my baby, but you're a grown Colored woman. I been eyeing you Tracy. You got a head on your shoulders, but there's so much you've yet to learn. You never stopped to think that the Sisters were gonna hit the roof, when they finally came to grips with the jobs you expect them to do. Realizing if they don't pick up their end they can very well be reponsible for a life. A life Tracy. Nor did you think they'd be tearin' at one another and you, when they finally came round to that. This ain't never been no comedy. None of us have ever been involved in anything like this. And it's showing. Our lives are on the line. And this ain't almost over. From now until you're six feet under you got to think. 'Specially when you tell somebody they might have to die in the name of your creation.

TRACY. Momma . . .

STELLA. I'm gon' get that rest you said we all needed.

TRACY. Momma I love you.

STELLA. That ain't never been the problem. (SHE *turns to walk, stops*) Then again, maybe it has. (SHE *EXITS*)

TRACY. This is my mission. Mine. My years, my

sweat. And I will do it. Even if I have to do it myself. I will do it. And nothing and no one's gonna take it away from me. Not Momma. Not even myself. I will.

ACT TWO

The scene begins in the blackout. STELLA'S *home. We hear the* WOMEN *singing one verse of the song "Steal Away." Once the singing is over lights come up. We see the* WOMEN *decked out in gangster suits and low brim hats.* THEY *are seated and standing in frozen tableau looking very much like gansters. After a beat or two of silence* BLU, *looking out the window, speaks.*

BLU. What's the time?
REDD. (*Pocketwatch*) Five of—
BLU. (*Looking out window*) Could be my imagination, but it sure is black as a dog's paw out there.

(SUDY *hums "Walks in the Light"*)

JADE. Let's all sing. (*Silence.* SUDY *stops humming*) Never mind.
TRACY. (*ENTERS carrying violin case*) Two minutes. We can start.
JADE. Two minutes so fast?
SUDY. Time can scoot.
JADE. Two minutes, you sure?
BLU. Don't start that.
STELLA. Two minutes is time 'nuff for a prayer.
REDD. Just don't make it a sad.
TRACY. Minute and a half.

STELLA. Let's gather. MAY THE LORD WATCH 'WEEN ME AND THEE WHILE WE ARE ABSENT ONE FROM THE OTHER. AMAN.

WOMEN. Aman.

TRACY. Time check?

REDD. Sixty seconds.

TRACY. All right women. The clocks ticking. We're ready. (TRACY *looks around*) Are you ready Sudy?

SUDY. As I'll ever be.

TRACY. You all right Bluiah?

BLU. Everything's under control.

TRACY. You packed tight Jade?

JADE. (*Touches her equipment*) Got it all.

TRACY. My partner?

REDD. Partner. (*Looks at watch*) 10 o'clock. We're on.

TRACY. Let's go.

(THEY *EXIT*. TRACY *and* STELLA *give each other a silent pause.* TRACY *then EXITS as* STELLA *behind* HER *closes door and turns off light. In the blackout we hear footsteps, car doors opening and shutting then a 1930s engine takes us to the scene of the bank. This scene is in darkness except for some of the* WOMEN *carrying flashlights.* WOMEN *are now in the process of breaking and entering. There is the constant sound of voices, shoes, keys, wire snapping.*)

TRACY. Sudy, your post.

STELLA. Be careful now.

SUDY. Don't fret 'bout a thing.

REDD. 10:30 Tracy.

SUDY. Just hurry and get back out.

TRACY. We're gone. Follow my voice. We all here?

WOMEN. (*Whispers*) Yes.

TRACY. Here's the door. Jade. (SHE *opens door to bank*)

JADE. So far so good.

TRACY. Light.

REDD. All clear. Move in. (*We hear them enter bank*)

TRACY. Picture the map and everything will be all right. Stay tight. Keep moving, stay tight. Follow the light. Two, three, four, five feet and and ... the vault should be to our right.

JADE. To our right ...

REDD. 10:32 Tracy.

TRACY. Hold it. This is it.

STELLA. It is?

JADE. It's so big.

TRACY. This is the vault.

REDD. 10:35.

TRACY. C'mon Jade find the wires.

JADE. Wait a minute ... wait a minute.

REDD. You see the wires? (*No answer*)

STELLA. Do you? (*Pause*)

JADE. Here they are. (*We hear clipping*) They're dead. I'm done. Go 'head Tracy.

TRACY. Quiet now.

STELLA. SHHHHHH.

TRACY. Didn't catch. One more again.

(*Pause*)

REDD. Anything?

TRACY. Wait, no.

JADE. No?

STELLA. Give it a chance.

REDD. Minute an' a half to go.

TRACY. All right. All right, here we go.

JADE. Tracy ... ?

STELLA. Shhhhh.

TRACY. Something's wrong. What am I doing wrong?

REDD. One minute.

TRACY. Yeah. To the right hold, left hold and r-r-right . . .

REDD. I heard something.

TRACY. Here it comes, it's coming its—

(*Massive alarm goes off*)

TRACY. Oh my God!

WOMEN. Screams/general confusion/panic.

TRACY. Alarm system, another alarm system!

REDD. We gotta get outta here. We gotta run.

TRACY. NO NO NO NO . . .

STELLA. Oh God Tracy, stop it, stop that thing!

REDD. She won't answer.

STELLA. (*We hear* HER *slap* TRACY) Damnit child. What should we do? You hear me?

REDD. Help us!

TRACY. I . . . we.

REDD. What?

STELLA. Talk!

JADE. Give me some light.

STELLA. Tracy! Tracy!

JADE. Give me some light!

REDD. What?

JADE. I think I see it. I think I can clip the wire—

REDD. Do it, do it!

STELLA. Tracy, what should— (*The wire is cut and alarm dies out*)

STELLA. Redd get Sudy.

STELLA. Go on! (SHE *EXITS*) What about us? Talk Tracy!

TRACY. Stuff the bags full. When Sudy—

SUDY. What the devil is—

TRACY. Stuff the bags. Did you see anyone?

SUDY. No. But they're comin'.

TRACY. Ah time check?

STELLA. Answer her!

REDD. 10:40, 10:40.

TRACY. It's enough.

STELLA. What?

TRACY. Momma you and Jade go back to the car. Sudy take my bag and cover for them. If Redd and I aren't out in 30 seconds leave—

SUDY. Leave . . . ?

STELLA. We're not leaving no one.

TRACY. We don't have time, go now.

STELLA. You, Redd and Jade go. I'll clean up here.

SUDY. Get going. We're staying.

TRACY. No! No!

SUDY. Get her outta here. Give us 15 seconds or leave! Don't argue.

REDD. Get up Tracy.

TRACY. Oh God no, no Momma!

SUDY. Take her!

(*We hear* REDD *and* JADE *taking* TRACY *as* SHE *fights to stay calling Momma . . . Momma . . .* THEY *EXIT*)

STELLA. Bail it Sudy, faster, faster, faster.

SUDY. This one's stuffed.

STELLA. Mine is getting there. Look around. Did we leave anything. Did we?

SUDY. No. Now let's—

STELLA. —say positive. Light check it.

SUDY. Positive, positive now c'mon Stella. Kill the light.

STELLA. You first.

SUDY. Oh heavens.

STELLA. Faster, c'mon, c'mon, c'mon.

(*We hear the horn beep three times.*)

SUDY. That's the signal. Let's go!

STELLA. You see the car? Where's the car? Where is it?

SUDY. I don't . . . I don't see it.

STELLA. Where are they?

SUDY. There! There they are. Get down. You first, I'll cover.

STELLA. Oh my heart. Here I go—1-2-3.

SUDY. No Stella! It's the police!

STELLA. What?

SUDY. Stella . . . Stella . . .

STELLA. They're gone. They left us.

BLACKOUT

SCENE 4

Return to STELLAS. *When lights rise* JADE *is looking out the window.* BLU *is standing.* REDD *ENTERS from kitchen.* TRACY *is pacing. There are two money bags on the table, one money bag on the sofa.)*

REDD. What are y'all doing? We still have to keep on schedule. Move it!

BLU. I told you, I'm not taking another step 'till somebody tells me what in the hell happened in there. Somebody tell me!

TRACY. *(Dazed)* You . . . you have to take off your suit. Take off your suit and turn the radio . . . (TRACY *turns on the radio*)

BLU. I'm talking to you TracyAda. Why did that alarm go off? Why?

JADE. I cut those wires. I know I did. Everything

was suposed to do I did. You didn't tell me 'bout those others. You didn't Tracy. You didn't. Oh where are they? (JADE *paces and occasionally peers out window*)

TRACY. We, we must continue to, to (*To* BLU) take your suit off. You must—

(TRACY *trys to remove* HER *jacket.* BLU *grabs* TRACY *and begins shaking* HER *about.* REDD *comes between* THEM)

BLU. If we don't panic the going won't get tough, huh? This will work, huh?

REDD. Stop it Bluiah! Let her go!

BLU. Get offa me Redd!

REDD. Let her go!

BLU. (*Still holding onto* TRACY) Tracy, you stay the hell away from me 'till Stella and Sudy walk through them doors. Stay the hell away. And so help you if they don't, 'cause I won't be responsible.

REDD. Let her go Buelah, let her go! Now listen to me. Everyone! We are going to continue. They will be here.

BLU. How do you know? Can you tell me where they're at right now? Can you? Are they alive, are they dead? Are they in jail? Well tell me?

REDD. Buelah we are here and we must go on. That's all I know. They will be here. Now pick up those bags and put them away.

BLU. I'm not moving.

NEWS VOICE. Just in . . . there has been a robbery at the Chicago Savings & Loan Local Bank. (REDD *turns the radio up*) Nearly three quarters of the money was stolen. It is believed to be the biggest robbery in the area so far. The authorities are beginning to gather clues. However no definite word as to who may be responsible. Again Chicago Savings & Loan Bank has been robbed. Now the weather, it's a clear night, stars . . .

(There is a loud police-like bang on the door. The WOMEN *freeze. We suddenly hear a voice.)*

STELLA. Tracy! Tracy open up!

*(*STELLA *and* SUDY *fall in out of breath, looking ragged.* THEY *each carry two money bags.)*

SUDY. Help us.

(The WOMEN *dash for* THEM *disarming the money bags)*

BLU. Thank God you're alive.
REDD. *(To* TRACY*)* Get some water.
SUDY. Get me some spirits.
JADE. Take off their jackets.
BLU. Are y'all all right? Are you? Leaving you both . . . I almost died.
STELLA. So did we.
SUDY. What you doing in your uniform?
BLU. I'll change now.
JADE. Thank God, thank God.

*(*TRACY *arrives with drinks in shot glasses.)*

BLU. I wasn't gonna leave y'all. You know I wouldn't.
SUDY. You did what we said.
STELLA. Please put the bags away.

*(*JADE *takes up the two money bags on table.* BLU *takes one on sofa.)*

REDD. Oh yes, let's keep going.
SUDY. Let's go change.
JADE. Y'all need any help?
STELLA. No. Put the bags up.
BLU. Stella . . . We got 'bout 4 bags there.

STELLA. Maybe.

BLU. This makes 5. Let's . . . let's let two be for us.

SUDY. What?

TRACY. Buelah . . .

JADE. Charity begins at home.

SUDY. Y'all must be going into after shock.

STELLA. Is that your excuse?

REDD. Excuse? We don't need no excuse. We owe this to ourselves. (REDD *picks up a money bag*)

TRACY. Redd . . .

SUDY. Oh we do?

REDD. Yes we do.

JADE. You know as well as me we coulda been killed. I was so scared.

STELLA. And what about us?

BLU. What would it hurt? Just a small cut for ourselves. Stella we need this money. Every last one of us, including yourself needs this money. Nobodies talkin' 'bout luxury.

REDD. She's right and you know it.

JADE. I really don't see what it would hurt neither, I don't see.

SUDY. Oh the devils dancin' tonight.

REDD. Sudy, there's nothin' wrong with it . . . Just like Buelah said, we don't see what—

STELLA. Neither did Judas Iscariot 'till it was too late. The only grace we have in getting this money is that it's ours in the spirit that we're gonna make something honorable of it. But just as sure as you're born, the moment we turn away from that spirit is the time we won't have nothin'. And we will have to pay for it dearly.

REDD. That's the chance we have to take, 'cause I'm takin' what's mine Stella. And this is mine.

TRACY. We don't have to bow to the devil. We've won. We've got the money to send at least 6 or 7 girls to college. Yes I was scared, but we've come this far as sisters in spirits. Let's keep on going together. Redd?

Please Jade? Blu?

(*Each* WOMAN *reluctantly gives* TRACY *her bag*)

NEWS VOICE. Just in. Clues are beginning to gather surrounding the night robbery at the Chicago Savings & Loan Bank apparently it is the work of Dillenger and new partner Andy Johnson, just sprung from prison. It is believed to be the first robbery attempted at night. Allegedy performed so authorities would not recognize Johnson. A plan now failing. Again clues are forming that Dillenger and new partner Andy Johnson are being sought.
    JADE. They think it's Dillenger . . .
    REDD. Not us . . .
    BLU. Not us . . .
    REDD. It's happening, it's happening then.

(WOMEN *rejoice.*)

    TRACY. And now, women, about this other plan I've got.
    WOMEN. What?!

END

PROPERTY FURNITURE

Tracy and Stella's Bedroom

Bed (1)
Bureau with mirror
Comb and brush set on bureau
Perfume bottle on bureau
Small floor rug
Small table with water basin and pitcher

Front Room Area

Large sitting chair
Sofa (1)
Loveseat (1)
Floor lamp (1)
Small table with small lamp and radio
Coat tree

Dining Area

Large table with six chairs
Break-front

PROPERTY LIST

ACT ONE, SCENE 1

Comb and brush set
Handkerchief
Snuff cup or can
Map (of bank)
Gift wrapped book
Large "WELCOME HOME TRACYADA" sign
Balloons and strings
Chocolate cake
Cake knife
Cake plates and cups (6) on dining table
Cloth napkins (6) on dining table
Cake forks (6) on dining table
Punch bowl

ACT ONE, SCENE 2

Hand held folding fan (Bluiah's)
Pan of rolls (3)
Cheese cloths (7 pieces)
Pie pans (4)
Brown paper bags (7)
Bootleg bottle
Glass (1)

ACT THREE, SCENE 1

Pocket watch

A long pointing stick for map
Ledger book
Cleaning cloths (5)
Medium size brown cloth bag
    for carrying equipment (1)
Handguns (2)
Rifles (2)
Flashlights (4)
Wire cutters (1)
Money bags (5)
Pants with needle and thread
Shot glasses and tray (5)

COSTUME LIST

Stella

Stylish brown sequined dress
Brown hat
Pearl necklace and earrings
Lace handkerchief
Brown shoes
Printed maroon dress
Brown handbag
1930s man's tailored 3-piece suit
Man's brown shoes
Man's brown low brim hat
Dark shirt and tie

TracyAda

Cream colored ribbon tied dress
Pair of eyeglasses
Brown shoes
Straw shoes
Beige dress
1930s pin-stripe 3-piece man's tailored navy and white
    suit
Navy low brim hat
Dark shirt and tie

Sudy

Two-piece navy and white dress

Navy hat
Dark gloves
Black shoes
Faded red printed dress
Apron
Light brown 3-piece 1930s man's tailored suit
Dark brown low brim hat
Dark shirt and tie
Brown men's shoes

Bluiah

Beige dress
Beige hat
Beige shawl
Gloves
Beige shoes
Brown hand bag
Violet dress
Pearl necklace
Brown 1930s 3-piece man's tailored suit
Brown shoes (man's)
Dark shirt and tie
Brown low brim hat

Renita

Red dress and matching jacket
Black shoes
Black hat
Black handbag
Necklace and earrings
Man's tailored maroon suit
Man's brown low brim hat
Brown shoes

Dark shirt and tie

Jade

Green dress
Beige hat
Black handbag
Green printed dress
Apron
Black shoes
Brown 1930s man's tailored 3-piece suit
Brown shoes
Brown low brim hat

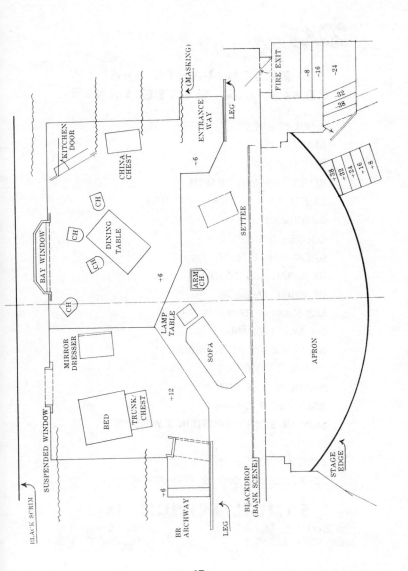

Plays FOR

BLACK CASTS and
BLACK and WHITE CASTS

AMEN CORNER

BLACKS, The

BLOOD KNOT

BLUES FOR MR. CHARLIE

CEREMONIES IN DARK OLD MEN

DUTCHMAN

GOLDEN BOY

GREAT WHITE HOPE, The

IN ABRAHAM'S BOSOM

IN WHITE AMERICA

MOON ON A RAINBOW SHAWL

MY SWEET CHARLIE

NO PLACE TO BE SOMEBODY

PURLIE VICTORIOUS

RAISIN IN THE SUN

ROLL SWEET CHARIOT

SIGN IN SIDNEY BRUSTEIN'S WINDOW

SLAVE

TAKE A GIANT STEP

TO BE YOUNG, GIFTED AND BLACK

SAMUEL FRENCH, Inc.

25 West 45th St.   7623 Sunset Blvd.
NEW YORK 10036   HOLLYWOOD 90046

#43

POOR BITOS

By JEAN ANOUILH, *translated by* LUCIENNE HILL

DRAMA

10 males, 3 females, 1 child—Interior

The French master of time and its illusions presents us in his latest play with a group of patricians gathered for a party in the vaulting room of an old chateau. We are quickly disabused of any notion that this is to be just another gay party a la dolce vita. For also invited is a literal, by-the-numbers, and intransigent prosecutor named Bitos whom they all detest. He is to them the reincarnation of Robespierre; and through a change of coats and the dramatic legerdermain of Anouilh the party recreates the time of Robespierre and the French Revolution before returning to the humiliating harshness of the present. "Never has Anouilh exposed mankind with such caustic candor; and the device by which he accomplishes this is a bitter and brilliant tragic-comedy."—*N.Y. World-Telegram & Sun.* "He reminds us that man is unchangingly erring, flawed man. Theatrical mastery. He weaves reality and make-believe into a subtle web that intensifies the reality."—*N.Y. Times.*

(Royalty, $50-$25.)

IN WHITE AMERICA

By MARTIN B. DUBERMAN

HISTORY

3 negro (2 male, 1 female)—3 white (2 male, 1 female)
Platform stage; musical interludes

An enactment from the actual records in the United States by a history professor, this is the continuously absorbing story of the negro from slave-trade times to Little Rock. Winner of the Vernon-Rice-Drama Desk Award. Here in a very gem of a letter are revealed the heart and soul of a runaway slave in reply to a master who has asked him to return. Here is the mournful account of a molested, widowed woman, and of her crippled baby, and the Ku Klux Klan. Here, too, is the moving speech by a southern senator in justification of lynching, the zenith of eloquent emotionalism. Altogether, a beautifully arranged enactment, with scenes of tremendous emotional power that will long endure.

(Royalty, $35-$25.)

A RAISIN IN THE SUN

By LORRAINE HANSBERRY

DRAMA

7 men, 3 women, 1 child—Interior

A Negro family is cramped in a flat on the south side of Chicago. They are a widow, her son (a chauffeur), his wife, his sister, and his little boy. The widow is expecting a $10,000 insurance settlement on her husband's death, and her son is constantly begging her to give him the money so that he can become co-owner of a liquor store. He wants to quit chauffeuring, to become a business man, and to be able to leave his son a little bit more than his own father, a brick-layer, had left him: this is the only way a Negro can continue to improve his lot. The widow, meantime, has placed a down-payment on a house where they can have sunlight, and be rid of roaches. The despair of the young husband is intense. His mother reluctantly turns over the remaining $6500 to him, as head of the house. He invests in the liquor store, his partner absconds, and his dream is forever dead. A representative from the better (white) neighborhood, into which they planned to move, calls on them and offers to reimburse them handsomely for their investment. But our young man now realizes that a little bit of dignity is all he can ever count on, and he plans to move his family to the new house.

(Royalty, $50-$25.)

PURLIE VICTORIOUS

By OSSIE DAVIS

COMEDY

6 men, 3 women—Exterior, 2 comp.

By taking all the cliches of plays, about the lovable old south and the love that existed between white masters and colored slaves, Ossie Davis has compounded a constantly comic play. Purlie Victorious has come back to his shabby cabin to announce that he will reacquire the local church and ring the freedom bell. There is an inheritance due to a colored cousin, which would be sufficient to buy the church, but unfortunately it also is controlled by the white-head plantation colonel. Purlie Victorious tries to send a newcomer to the colonel to impersonate the heiress, not only is she found out, but the colonel makes a pass at her. Eventually the church is recovered, services are again held in it, and the freedom bell rings. It is the dialogue, though, that makes the events so uproarious ("Are you trying to get non-violent with me, boy?") or human ("Oh, child, being colored can be a lot of fun when they ain't nobody looking"). There's uncommonly good sense in such a line as the one delivered to Purlie when he was about to beat the colonel with the colonel's well-worn bullwhip: "You can't do wrong just because it's right."

(Royalty, $50-$25.)

The Tandem Library

A Selection of 20 Plays from

All in the Family

Sanford and Son

Good Times

Maude

For details of titles available and royalty fees apply to Samuel French, Inc.

DATE DUE			